JIMMY CARTER
LIBRARY AND MUSEUM

Amy Margaret

The Rosen Publishing Group's

PowerKids Press™

New York

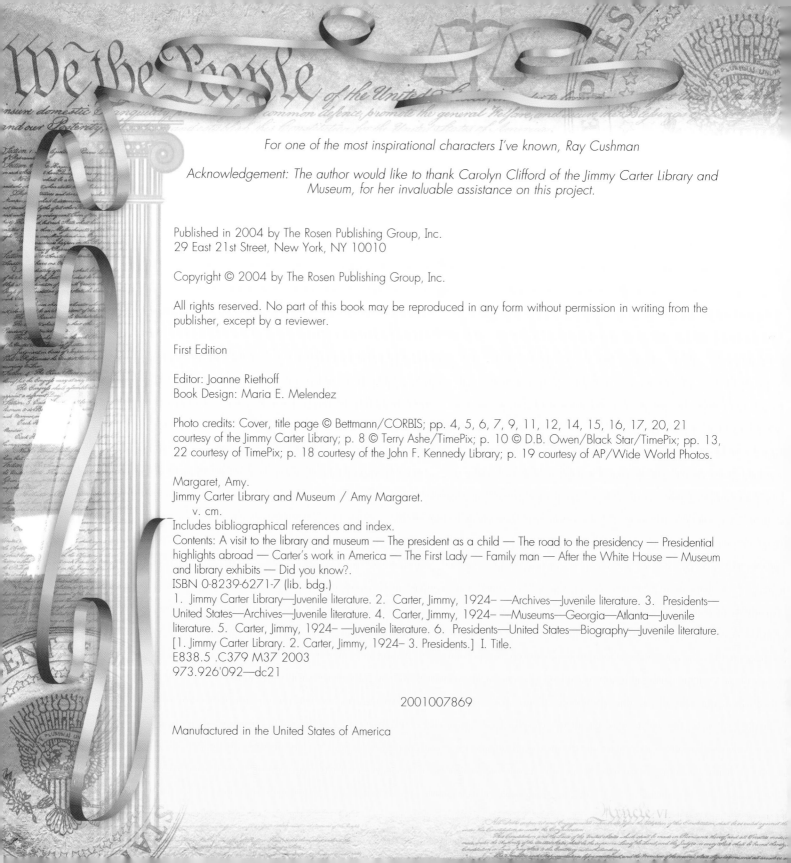

For one of the most inspirational characters I've known, Ray Cushman

Acknowledgement: The author would like to thank Carolyn Clifford of the Jimmy Carter Library and Museum, for her invaluable assistance on this project.

Published in 2004 by The Rosen Publishing Group, Inc.
29 East 21st Street, New York, NY 10010

First Edition

Editor: Joanne Riethoff
Book Design: Maria E. Melendez

Photo credits: Cover, title page © Bettmann/CORBIS; pp. 4, 5, 6, 7, 9, 11, 12, 14, 15, 16, 17, 20, 21 courtesy of the Jimmy Carter Library; p. 8 © Terry Ashe/TimePix; p. 10 © D.B. Owen/Black Star/TimePix; pp. 13, 22 courtesy of TimePix; p. 18 courtesy of the John F. Kennedy Library; p. 19 courtesy of AP/Wide World Photos.

CONTENTS

A VISIT TO THE LIBRARY AND MUSEUM

The grounds of the Jimmy Carter Library and Museum have a Japanese garden (above). This garden has Japanese buildings and sculptures. It also has a fish pond.

The Jimmy Carter Library and Museum opened on October 1, 1986. This day was Jimmy Carter's sixty-second birthday. The building is located in Atlanta, Georgia. From 80,000 to 100,000 visitors go to the library and museum each year.

The library and the museum are in the same building. The museum is on the first floor, and the library is on the second floor. The Carter Center is separate from the library and museum, even though it is on the same grounds. The Carter Center is devoted to Jimmy and Rosalynn Carter's personal projects and is not open to the public.

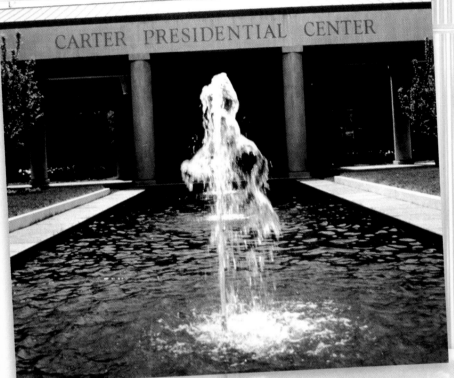

The Carter Presidential Center is the name of the complex in which you'll find the Jimmy Carter Library and Museum and the Carter Center. Both organizations are in the same place, but they are run by different groups.

The library and the museum took two years to build and cost about $26 million. Woods, ponds, and gardens surround the building. The Carter Library and Museum holds more than 27 million papers, as well as historical materials from the time that Carter was president of the United States.

THE PRESIDENT AS A CHILD

Jimmy Carter was born on October 1, 1924, in a small town in Georgia called Plains. Jimmy's father, James Earl Carter Sr., grew peanuts, fruits, and vegetables. He also raised animals for their milk, meat, and wool. Many of his products were sold in the grocery store that he owned.

Jimmy worked on the farm, carrying wood, gathering eggs, and milking cows. As did most of their neighbors, the Carters lived without electricity or a telephone. Jimmy loved fishing and reading books. He attended Georgia Southwestern College and Georgia Institute of Technology. He entered the U.S. Naval Academy in 1943.

This picture, taken in the 1920s, shows Jimmy Carter (right) with his father and two sisters, Gloria and Ruth. Jimmy's father, James Earl Carter Sr., held jobs in many different fields, including farming, sales, and government. Jimmy's mother, Lillian, was a registered nurse.

The Jimmy Carter Library and Museum has many pictures from Jimmy's childhood, including a baby picture and his high school basketball team picture (above). Jimmy is in the top row, wearing the uniform labeled "10."

THE ROAD TO THE PRESIDENCY

Jimmy Carter **graduated** from the U.S. Naval Academy in 1946. He married Rosalynn Smith one month later. He worked for the U.S. Navy and became a **submariner** in New York State. Carter's father died in 1953, so Jimmy and Rosalynn moved back to Georgia to run the family business, Carter's Warehouse. In Georgia, Carter became involved in local **politics**. In 1962, he was elected to the Georgia **senate**. In 1971, Carter became Georgia's **governor**. At the end of 1974, Carter announced that he would run for president of the United States. Carter won the presidency, and he took office in 1977.

A newly elected president and his family are driven from the U.S. Capitol to the White House. Thousands of people gather to see the presidential family pass by. The Carters started the parade in cars. Unlike in previous presidential parades, the cars stopped. Carter, his wife, and their children got out of the cars to walk the 1 ½ miles (2.5 km) to the White House.

When Carter announced that he was going to run for president of the United States, most people had never heard of him. He and Rosalynn traveled across the country to meet the American people. Shown here is the Campaign Room display. Signs and bumperstickers read "Say Something Nice About Jimmy" and "A New Spirit, A New Commitment, A New America."

THE PRESIDENT OVERSEAS

Anwar el Sadat and Menachem Begin hug each other at the signing of the peace treaty on March 26, 1979. President Carter is shown on the right clapping with approval at the two leaders' show of affection.

In 1977, Israel and the United States got along well. Since 1948, Israel had fought four major wars with Egypt. Carter wanted to help Israel and Egypt be at peace. In 1978, he invited Egyptian president Anwar el Sadat and Israeli **prime minister** Menachem Begin to **Camp David** to discuss their differences. They spent 13 days arguing and writing a plan for peace. The two leaders went back to their homelands while details continued to be worked out. It took another six months before Sadat and Begin could agree on the **treaty**. On March 26, 1979, the peace treaty was signed. This event is shown in an **exhibit** at the museum.

PEACE IN THE MIDDLE EAST

Shown here is the Camp David display. Carter was awarded the 2002 Nobel Peace Prize. He won the prize for his efforts to find peaceful solutions to conflicts between nations, including his work on the Israel-Egypt Peace Treaty, as shown here.

CARTER'S WORK IN AMERICA

Robert Ode was one of the hostages in Iran. He donated his journal (above) to the Carter Library. It was the journal that he kept while he was a prisoner in Iran. The entire diary is available for the public to read. The above entry is from October 30, 1980. It was his 362nd day of being held hostage.

Carter also had his work cut out for him at home. Soon after Carter entered office in 1977, many states suffered a gas shortage. He created an energy plan. In October 1978, **Congress** passed the first part of the president's energy plan. In this plan, the use of coal and **solar power** would be **rewarded**. Carter continued to work on this energy plan. It became law in 1980.

In November 1979, **terrorists** held 52 **hostages** in the American **embassy** in Iran. Carter spent the rest of his presidency trying to get them released, but the hostages were not released until January 20, 1981. That was the day Ronald Reagan became president.

Carter was on the cover of the April 25, 1977, issue of Time magazine. The energy crisis in the United States in the 1970s was considered by some to be President Carter's "first big test." The crisis got so bad that sometimes cars would be lined up for many blocks waiting for fuel at gas stations.

THE FIRST LADY

Eleanor Rosalynn Smith Carter grew up in Plains, Georgia. She graduated from high school as **valedictorian** of a class of 11 students.

When Jimmy Carter was the governor of Georgia, Rosalynn wanted him to support **mental**-health programs. In the White House, she continued her support of mental-health programs. Throughout the museum, there are photographs that show her working on her mental-health projects.

During the White House years, the First Lady also worked to get the **Equal Rights Amendment** (ERA) passed. This amendment would have strengthened women's rights in the United States.

When Carter was running for the presidency in 1976, he told reporters that Rosalynn was not a supporter of the women's rights movement. Rosalynn read this in a newspaper and called reporters to tell them that she was indeed a supporter of equal rights for women.

This photograph was taken on April 20, 1977. It shows Rosalynn speaking at a meeting regarding mental health. Her activity in the Commission on Mental Health resulted in the Mental Health Systems Act of 1980. This act helped to better the mental health centers in individual communities, so that people with mental illnesses could stay close to home and out of hospitals.

FAMILY MAN

In 1947, the Carters had their first child, John William, who was called Jack. James Earl III, nicknamed Chip, and Donnel Jeffrey, called Jeff, followed over the next five years. In 1967, when Jeff was 15 years old, Rosalynn gave birth to Amy Lynn.

By the time the Carters reached the White House in 1977, the three boys were grown and had families of their own. Chip and Jeff, along with their families, came to live in the White House with President Carter, Rosalynn, and Amy. There are many family photographs on display at the library and the museum for visitors and researchers to see.

This picture was taken on September 6, 1980. Carter is shown here with two of his grandchildren. Jason stands and waves to the camera, and Sarah sits on a bicycle.

Amy is shown here with Mary Fitzpatrick, the Carters' housekeeper. Amy was 10 years old when she moved to the White House, and she didn't want to leave her friends and her school. Mary helped Amy get used to her new home.

The Carters brought a lot of people with them when they moved into the White House. Here Carter is shown with his family.

LIFE AFTER THE WHITE HOUSE

Soon after he lost the 1980 election, Jimmy Carter wanted to create a place where unfriendly groups could work out their problems. The idea for the Carter Center was born. The center is on the same site as the Jimmy Carter Library and Museum, but the two organizations are run separately.

Carter has personally worked with world leaders to free thousands of **political prisoners**. The Global 2000 program at the Carter Center provides food for the hungry in several countries, such as Ethiopia and Sudan. From his time in the presidency to today, Jimmy Carter has worked to bring peace to nations and help to the poor.

In 1999, President Bill Clinton presented Jimmy and Rosalynn Carter with the Presidential Medal of Freedom (above). This award was given largely because of the work the Carters have done through the Carter Center. For example, since its opening, the center has prevented 11 million people in Africa and Latin America from getting an illness called river blindness.

Since his presidency, Jimmy and Rosalynn Carter have both been active. Here Carter is shown helping to build housing for people in need. This project was sponsored by an organization called Habitat for Humanity.

Here Rosalynn talks about her book, Helping Someone with Mental Illness. This photograph was taken on May 19, 1998.

LIBRARY AND MUSEUM EXHIBITS

The museum has several exhibits that teach visitors about Carter's presidency. Several of the gifts that President Carter received from other country leaders are on display. One of the most interesting gifts is an oil painting of President Carter, given to him by the president of Mexico. It is a picture of Carter, but there are smaller pictures within the large painting. For instance his hair is made up of the 50 state flags of the United States.

The museum also features from two to four temporary exhibits each year. One of these was the *Little White House*, a 20-foot (6-m) by 60-foot (18-m) copy of America's White House.

On exhibit at the library is a copy of the Crown of St. Stephen, the national symbol for Hungary. At the end of World War II, Hungary gave the crown to the U.S. Army for safekeeping. In 1977, Carter returned the crown to Hungary. In 1998, a copy of the crown was given to Carter by the president of the Republic of Hungary.

If you look closely at this painting of Jimmy Carter, you can see all the different images. His hair is made up of flags. His tie and suit jacket are made up of buildings. His right hand is made up of ships and their masts, and his left hand is made up of trucks. This painting was given to Carter by José Lopez Portillo, the president of Mexico. It was painted by Octavio Ocampo.

Jimmy Carter was chosen as Time magazine's Man of the Year in 1976. He appeared on the cover of Time magazine at least 33 times!

DID YOU KNOW?

Here are some fun facts to share with friends about the thirty-ninth U.S. president:

Jimmy Carter was the first president born in a hospital!

As a boy, Jimmy gave his mother's diamond **engagement ring** to his first-grade teacher. He said to her, "My Daddy can always buy Momma another one."

Jimmy Carter was the first president to have graduated from the U.S. Naval Academy in Maryland.

Carter's favorite drink is buttermilk.

Coca-Cola was the only soft drink served in the White House during Carter's presidency.

GLOSSARY

Camp David (KAMP DAY-vid) A place of retreat for the current U.S. president and anyone he wants to invite.

Congress (KON-gres) The part of the U.S. government that makes laws.

embassy (EHM-buh-see) The official home and office of those working for their home government in a foreign country.

engagement ring (en-GAYJ-ment RING) A ring given when two people decide to marry.

Equal Rights Amendment (EE-kwul RYTS uh-MEND-ment) An addition or change to the Constitution that would have given women the same rights as men.

exhibit (ig-ZIH-bit) Objects or pictures set out for people to see.

governor (GUH-vuh-nur) An official elected as head of a state.

graduated (GRA-joo-ayt-ed) Finished a course in school.

hostages (HOS-tij-ez) People held as prisoners until some demand is agreed to.

mental (MEN-tuhl) Having to do with the mind.

political prisoners (puh-LIH-tih-kul PRIH-zun-erz) People who have been put in prison because they don't agree with their political leaders.

politics (PAH-lih-tiks) Having to do with elections and governments.

prime minister (PRYM MIH-nih-stur) The official head of a government with a parliament.

rewarded (rih-WARD-ed) To have been offered a payment for doing something.

senate (SEH-nit) A law-making part of the state or U.S. government.

solar power (SOH-ler POW-ur) Energy taken from the sun to heat homes or give power to machinery.

submariner (suhb-mah-REE-nur) A member of a submarine crew.

terrorists (TER-ur-ists) Those who commit violent acts to frighten people.

treaty (TREE-tee) A formal agreement, signed and agreed upon by each party.

valedictorian (vah-luh-dik-TOR-ee-un) The student with the highest grades in the class, who gives a speech at graduation.

INDEX

PRIMARY SOURCES

Pages 4–7, 9, 11–12, 14–17, 20–21: Pictures were obtained from the Jimmy Carter Library and Museum. **Page18:** Picture was obtained from the John F. Kennedy Library and Museum.

WEB SITES

Due to the changing nature of Internet links, PowerKids Press has developed an online list of Web sites related to the subject of this book. This site is updated regularly. Please use this link to access the list:
www.powerkidslinks.com/pl/jimclm/